Light

Q&A

Gina L. Hamilton

www.av2books.com

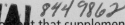
MAI 844 9862

AV² provides enriched content that supplements and complements this book. Weigl's AV² books strive to create inspired learning and engage young minds in a total learning experience.

Your AV² Media Enhanced books come alive with...

Audio
Listen to sections of the book read aloud.

Key Words
Study vocabulary, and complete a matching word activity.

Video
Watch informative video clips.

Quizzes
Test your knowledge.

Go to **www.av2books.com**, and enter this book's unique code.

Embedded Weblinks
Gain additional information for research.

Slide Show
View images and captions, and prepare a presentation.

BOOK CODE

N744708

AV² **by Weigl** brings you media enhanced books that support active learning.

Try This!
Complete activities and hands-on experiments.

...and much, much more!

Published by AV² by Weigl
350 5th Avenue, 59th Floor
New York, NY 10118
Website: www.av2books.com   www.weigl.com

Library of Congress Cataloging-in-Publication Data

Hamilton, Gina L.
[Light]
Light Q & A / Gina L. Hamilton.
     p. cm. — (Science discovery)
Originally published as Light. New York : Weigl Publishers, 2009.
Includes index.
Audience: 4-6.
ISBN 978-1-62127-415-5 (hardcover : alk. paper) — ISBN 978-1-62127-421-6 (pbk. : alk. paper)
1. Light—Juvenile literature. 2. Optics—Juvenile literature. 3. Children's questions and answers. I. Title. II. Title: Light questions & answers. III. Title: Light questions and answers.
QC360.H345 2013
535--dc23

                              2012039655

Printed in the United States of America, in North Mankato, Minnesota
1 2 3 4 5 6 7 8 9 0   17 16 15 14 13

062013
WEP040413B

Project Coordinator Aaron Carr   Designer Mandy Christiansen

Contents

What Is Light?

Light is a form of **electromagnetic energy**. This energy is made up of changing electric and **magnetic fields**. Light may be visible or invisible. Different types of visible and invisible light make up the **electromagnetic spectrum**. The tiny part of the electromagnetic spectrum that humans can see is called the visible light spectrum. Just as waves in water ripple out from their source, light can be thought of as a wave that spreads out in all directions from a light source, such as the Sun or a light bulb. Light gets dimmer as it moves farther away from its source. Light waves radiate, or travel, along straight lines called rays. This process is called radiation. The light people can see is only one type of radiation.

How Scientists Use Inquiry to Answer Questions

When scientists try to answer a question, they follow the process of scientific inquiry. They begin by making observations and asking questions. Then, they propose an answer to their question. This is called the hypothesis. The hypothesis guides scientists as they research the issue. Research can involve performing experiments or reading books on the subject. When the research is finished, scientists examine their results and review their hypothesis. Often, they discover that their hypothesis was incorrect. If this happens, they revise their hypothesis and go through the process of scientific inquiry again.

Process of Scientific Inquiry

Observation

Light makes objects visible, helps plants grow, and is a form of energy. Light is actually electromagnetic radiation. It is partly electric and partly magnetic. Not only is there visible light, but there is invisible light as well.

Have You Answered the Question?

The cycle of scientific inquiry never really ends. Once they have learned what the speed of light is, scientists might ask, "Can other objects travel at the speed of light?" The cycle of inquiry continues.

Research

Scientists have studied light and its properties for centuries. They started with basic questions such as "Where does light come from?" and "How does light travel?"

Results

Scientists have answered many questions about visible and invisible light. With each answer, scientists ask more questions. This leads to more research and experiments.

Hypothesis

Scientists continue to hypothesize about light, its properties, its effects, and its many uses. This leads them to conduct experiments and more research.

Experiment

Scientists can only observe visible light and its effects with the body's senses. They rely on research tools to conduct experiments. Scientists also use mathematics and technology to gain more information.

Why Is Light Important?

What would life on Earth be like without light and energy from the Sun? Light is essential to our existence. Without it, people would be unable to see anything, and most living things on Earth would not survive. Light from the Sun provides energy for life on Earth.

Most life on Earth depends on light and the relationship between plants and light. Plants turn sunlight into food through a process called **photosynthesis**. Photosynthesis is the first step in the food chain that connects almost all living things. Plants are a basic source of food because almost all animals eat plants, the products of plants, or other animals that eat plants. For example, cattle and other farm animals graze in fields of grass. Many people then eat meat and drink milk that comes from these animals.

In addition to its role in photosynthesis, another important aspect of sunlight is the warmth it provides. The Sun's energy keeps Earth at a temperature suitable for living things to survive.

❯ In additional to sunlight, most producers, such as grass and other plants, also need water and good soil in order to grow.

❮ On average, a cow weighing 1,000 pounds (454 kilograms) will eat 167 pounds (76 kg) of grass per day.

Digging Deeper

Your Challenge!

Obtain two small plants. Place one in a warm, sunny area. Place the other in a warm, shaded area where it will receive no direct sunlight. Give each plant 1 tablespoon of water every day at the same time. Record your observations daily for six days. What did you observe about the two plants? What conclusions can you make?

Summary

Sunlight is essential to life on Earth. The Sun provides energy and warmth.

Further Inquiry

Light from the Sun provides energy for life on Earth. Maybe we should ask:

How do we use light as energy?

How Do We Use Light as Energy?

Every day, the Sun provides Earth with large amounts of energy in the form of light. Scientists have made great strides in developing ways to capture this light. They have invented solar cells that collect light from the Sun to power equipment, light homes, and heat up water. These solar cells are also called photovoltaic cells. They work by changing light energy into electricity. When grouped in large panels, these cells can generate enough electricity to power houses, office buildings, and even entire communities.

Energy converted from sunlight is one of the most promising sources of **alternative energy**. Many researchers and people who are concerned about the environment believe that alternate sources of energy, such as solar energy, will help reduce pollution and the reliance upon fossil fuels, such as oil and gas. Today, most energy comes from burning coal, gas, and oil. These substances are known as fossil fuels because they were formed millions of years ago from the remains of prehistoric animals and plants. However, fossil fuels will not last forever. They also pollute the air when they burn. Sunlight remains one of the most promising sources of clean, **renewable energy**.

❮ Solar cells are used in areas that receive large amounts of sunlight all year round.

Your Challenge!

Place one bottle of water in direct sunlight and a second bottle of water away from direct sunlight. After one hour, measure the temperature of the water in each bottle. What did you find?

Summary

The Sun provides energy that people can use instead of fossil fuels. Using solar energy will help reduce pollution on Earth and provide a promising clean alternative energy source to fossil fuels.

Further Inquiry

Light from the Sun can be used to create electricity. However, light can be observed to travel in different ways. Maybe we should ask:

Is light a particle or a wave?

Is Light a Particle or a Wave?

Light acts like a wave. It also, however, acts like a particle. For centuries, scientists have debated whether light is a particle or a wave. Some ancient Greek scientists believed light was made of a stream of very small **particles**.

Sir Isaac Newton believed in this particle theory of light in the early 1700s. At about the same time, Christiaan Huygens came up with a different theory. He thought light acted more like a wave than a stream of particles. He saw that light spread out once it passed through a small opening. If the particle theory were correct, the light would remain in a beam as it passed straight through the opening. Over the years, scientists began to agree with Huygens' theory. By the 19th century, the wave theory had become the most accepted theory of the behavior of light.

In 1905, physicist Albert Einstein developed a different theory of light. He believed that light has some characteristics of a particle and some characteristics of a wave. This idea is known as the wave-particle duality theory. Einstein observed that, under certain circumstances, light waves behaved as though they were made of individual energy packets. These energy packets are known as **photons**. Einstein's revolutionary ideas went against hundreds of years of study and beliefs. They astonished scientists all over the world.

❯ Albert Einstein received the Nobel Prize for his discovery of the photoelectric effect. This law shows that light is made up of particles called photons.

Digging Deeper

Your Challenge!

Use a flashlight to investigate the way light travels. Cut a series of slits close together through a piece of paper or index card. Make the slits large enough for light to pass through. Then, in a dim or dark room, hold the flashlight so it shines through the slits in the paper. You may need to adjust the paper or index card and the flashlight in order to see the light effect. What do you observe?

Summary

At times, light behaves as a particle. At other times, it acts like a wave. This has become known as the wave-particle duality of light.

Further Inquiry

Studying light and its properties is difficult because light moves so quickly. Maybe we should ask:

How fast does light travel?

⌃ Light travels in a straight line, like a stream of particles. Light also spreads out in all directions, like a wave.

Q&A

How Fast Does Light Travel?

Light is the fastest thing in the universe. Light can travel around Earth seven times in one second. The Sun is 93 million miles (150 million kilometers) from Earth. It takes about eight minutes for light to travel from the Sun to Earth. In a **vacuum,** light travels at about 186,000 miles (299,792 km) per second.

The speed of light was discovered by Armand Fizeau in 1849. He timed it using a spinning cogwheel—a special wheel that had small teeth, or gaps, evenly spaced around its edge—and a mirror set up about 5.4 miles (8.6 km) away. Light passed through one gap between the teeth of the wheel as it traveled to the mirror and, if the wheel was turning quickly enough, through a neighboring gap on the way back. By knowing the speed of the wheel, Fizeau could calculate the speed of light as it traveled to the mirror and back.

Later, scientists wondered if light projected from the front of a moving train traveled at the speed of light plus the speed of the train. Physicist Albert Einstein learned the answer in 1905. Einstein discovered that the speed of light remains constant. It never changes, no matter the speed of the train. This is called Einstein's Special Theory of Relativity. A simple explanation of the special theory of relativity is that nothing travels faster than the speed of light. As an object approaches the speed of light, it becomes heavier and needs more energy to make it move. This means that even a tiny object would become infinitely heavy at the speed light, and it would need an infinite supply of energy to keep it moving at that speed.

❯ If an object traveled continuously at the speed of light for one year, it would cover a distance of over 5.8 trillion miles (9.5 trillion km).

Digging Deeper

Your Challenge!

Research how long it takes light from the Sun to reach the other planets in our solar system. Challenge yourself now by answering this question using the information in this section: If it takes eight minutes for light to travel 93 million miles (150 million km) from the Sun to Earth, how long will it take to travel 114 million miles (228 million km) from the Sun to Mars? Remember to convert seconds to minutes.

Summary

Light travels at 186,000 miles (299,792 km) per second. The speed of light is constant.

Further Inquiry

Light was first measured using visible light. There are also types of light that are invisible. Maybe we should ask:

What is invisible light?

What Is Invisible Light?

Visible light, the small group of light waves in the middle of the electromagnetic spectrum, is the type of light most familiar to humans. Objects such as the Sun and stars emit visible light, as well as invisible light. Invisible light is different forms of radiation on either side of the visible light spectrum. The **wavelengths** located on either side of the visible light spectrum are important. These wavelengths are too long or too short to be detected by the human eye. Even though most people never think about it, invisible light is everywhere.

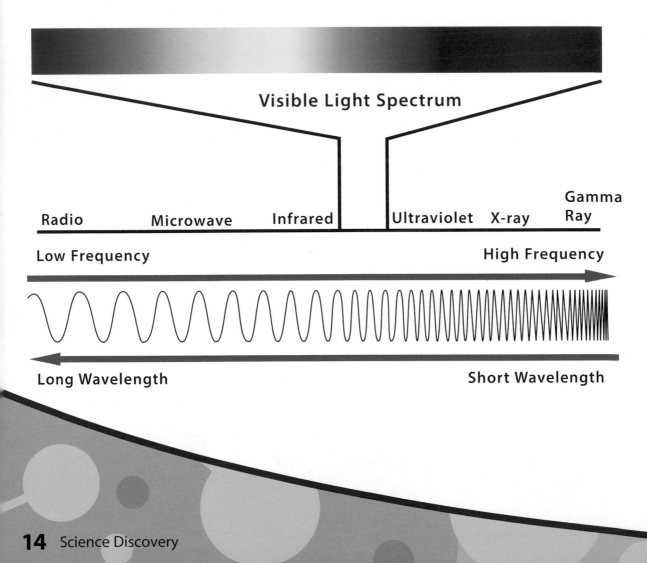

Visible Light Spectrum

Radio　　Microwave　　Infrared　　Ultraviolet　X-ray　Gamma Ray

Low Frequency　　　　　　　　　　High Frequency

Long Wavelength　　　　　　　　Short Wavelength

Radio waves are forms of invisible light. They have very long wavelengths and are at one end of the electromagnetic spectrum. They are used to send radio and television signals. Microwaves are also at this end of the spectrum and are often used for cooking and in radar technology. X-rays and gamma rays have very short wavelengths and are at the opposite end of the spectrum. These high-frequency waves are used mostly in medicine. For example, gamma rays are used to destroy cancer cells and sterilize, or clean, hospital equipment.

⌄ An x-ray is a form of electromagnetic radiation that can be used to take an image of the internal structures of the body.

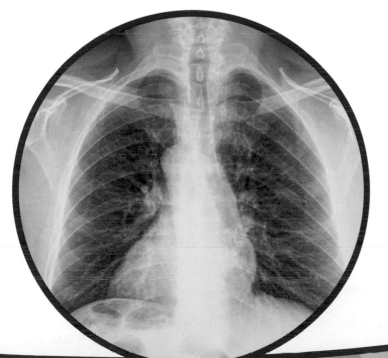

Your Challenge!

Research how invisible light is used in the medical field. Create a poster board or multimedia presentation showing how x-rays and gamma rays are used in hospitals. You can get a good start by researching "radiology" and "oncology."

Summary

The electromagnetic spectrum includes visible and invisible light. The wavelengths that make up the invisible light spectrum are used in a variety of tools and technologies.

Further Inquiry

Infrared is another important type of invisible light. It has many uses in science. Maybe we should ask:

What is infrared light?

What Is Infrared Light?

Infrared light is the part of the invisible light spectrum. It is found next to the red end of the visible light spectrum. Sir Frederick William Herschel discovered infrared light in 1800. He was the first person to discover that there were forms of light that human eyes cannot see.

Anything with a temperature gives off radiation. This radiation is in the form of infrared light. Infrared light cannot be seen by people, but it can be measured, and even felt. Very hot objects, such as hot coals, may not give off light that can be seen, but they give off infrared radiation that can be felt as heat. Even very cold objects, such as ice cubes, give off some infrared radiation.

Most people use infrared radiation every day without knowing it. Television and stereo remote controls use infrared technology. When a button is pressed on the remote control, it sends an infrared light signal. The television or stereo receives the signal and responds to it.

Infrared light is also used in computers to scan bar codes at the checkout counter in stores. Infrared technology is used in devices such as night-vision goggles. Most night-vision goggles are sensitive to the heat, or infrared radiation, produced by objects. Night-vision goggles enable people to see as well at night as they do during the day.

❯ Night-vision binoculars help people see objects at a distance when there is not enough light for regular binoculars to work.

▾ Infrared technology shows heat light colors, such as yellow or white. Cooler objects are dark colors, such as purple or black.

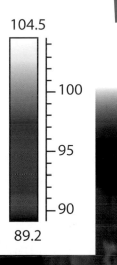

104.5

100

95

90

89.2

Digging Deeper

Your Challenge!

Infrared light technology is being used by scientists to learn more about the universe. Use the internet or library resources to research the NASA Spitzer Space Telescope. How does this telescope use infrared light to learn more about the universe?

Summary

Infrared light is part of the electromagnetic spectrum. It is often observed as heat. Infrared light is used in a wide variety of technologies, from television remote controls to computer scanners.

Further Inquiry

Most people use devices with infrared technology every day. Lasers are another commonly used light technology. Maybe we should ask:

What are lasers?

What Are Lasers?

Most light spreads out into a wide circle, strongest in the center of the circle and weakest at the outer edge of the circle. Light seen from the Sun, a lamp, or a flashlight is a mixture of many different wavelengths that, when mixed together, appear to be white. The wavelengths are all different, so they are incoherent, or out of step with one another. This spreads the light waves in all directions. Laser light does not do this. Laser light is all one wavelength and color, and all the waves are in step with one another. They are coherent.

> ❯ Laser is an acronym for "light amplification by stimulated emission of radiation."

Laser beams are created when **atoms** contained within a tube are stirred up by electricity. When the atoms are treated this way, they produce coherent light waves. Focusing these light waves with mirrors and **lenses** produces an intense beam of coherent light. This is a laser beam.

Lasers always travel in a straight line without spreading out. This means that they can be used in construction and other fields where a straight, accurate line is necessary for precise measurements. Laser light is also powerful tool in medicine because lasers can cut with precision. Laser light can be used to correct vision, drill teeth, and remove diseased tissue during surgery.

What Are Absorption, Reflection, and Transmission?

What happens to light when it hits an object? Does it bounce off, go inside the object, or go straight through? Do different objects cause light to react in different ways?

Just as a ball bounces off a wall or floor, light bounces off some objects. This is called reflection. Most uneven surfaces, such as clothing, paper, and skin, reflect light and scatter it in many directions. For example, if a person looks at their reflection in a piece of unpolished metal, which has an uneven surface, the image appears blurry or distorted.

❯ Reflection occurs when light waves encounter a surface or that does not absorb their energy. The waves bounce away from the surface and an image is produced.

Some objects are better reflectors than other objects. Smooth and shiny surfaces reflect light well. Perfectly smooth surfaces allow light to reflect evenly. Mirrors are nearly perfect reflectors. This means that almost all of the light that shines on a mirror reflects off it at the same angle.

Some surfaces take in light. This is called absorption. When light is absorbed, it is taken in and is unable to bounce back or reflect. Think about a black car and a white car on a hot, sunny day. Since black objects absorb light, the surface of the black car will be much hotter to the touch than the white car, which reflects light.

During transmission, light is not reflected or absorbed. When light is transmitted, it passes right through a surface or object. Clear glass is an example of a surface that transmits light.

Digging Deeper

Your Challenge!

To dig deeper into reflection:

1. Use a marker to draw a circle on an index card. Place the index card in the center of a desk or table.

2. Hold a piece of foil with the shiny side facing the card above the desk or table at a slight angle.

3. Shine a flashlight onto the shiny side of the foil. Try to get the light from the flashlight to reflect off the foil into the circle on the card.

What did you have to do to get the light to shine on the card?

Summary

When light strikes an object it is either absorbed by, reflected off, or transmitted through the object.

Further Inquiry

Objects cause light to react in different ways. Maybe we should ask:

Why do some objects cast shadows?

Why Do Some Objects Cast Shadows?

Why does a tree cast a shadow but a glass door does not? There are some objects that you can see through and some that you cannot. A transparent object allows most of the light it comes into contact with to pass through it. A goldfish bowl is transparent.

A translucent object allows some light to pass through it, but it does not allow enough light through so that objects can be seen clearly on the other side of it. The light changes direction many times and is scattered as it passes through. Therefore, objects cannot be seen clearly through translucent materials and appear fuzzy and unclear. Frosted glass and some plastics are examples of translucent materials.

Opaque objects, such as a solid structure, cast shadows. A brick wall is opaque. A person or a statue is also opaque. A shadow is the area behind an opaque object where light cannot reach. A shadow shows the outline of the object that is blocking the light.

An opaque object, such as a basketball, casts a shadow. The size of the shadow the ball casts shrinks as the ball is moved away from a light source. For example, if the basketball is near a light bulb, it casts a large shadow on the wall. If the ball is placed farther away from the light bulb, it blocks less light, so the shadow is smaller.

❯ Shadows can be used to tell time on a sundial. As the Sun moves through the sky, the shadow on the sundial moves and points to the correct time.

Digging Deeper

Your Challenge!

Research how to build your own sundial from common objects. Once your sundial is complete, use a watch and observe your sundial throughout the day to see how accurate it is.

Summary

Shadows are cast by objects when light cannot reach the surface on one side of the object. Light cannot bend around the object. The size of a shadow is directly related to the distance between the light source and the object.

Further Inquiry

Shadows are caused when light strikes an object and cannot transmit through it. Some materials allow light to pass through them easily. Maybe we should ask:

What is fiber optics?

What Is Fiber Optics?

Fiber optics cables are long strands of glass or plastic used to move information at high speeds across long distances. Fiber optic cables carry light instead of electricity. These cables are not affected by changes in the temperature, rain, cold, or virtually any other environmental condition.

Each fiber optic strand is as thin as a strand of human hair. Hundreds of thousands of fiber optic strands are placed together in bundles called optic cables. Sounds, images, and other information are changed into pulses of light. These pulses of light then travel through the fiber optic cables.

⌄ Fiber optic cables allow information to be sent around the world in less than a second.

A fiber optic strand, called the core, is covered by a transparent coating called cladding. Light usually transmits through transparent surfaces, but the cladding is designed to block the light, sending it back into the core. The light pulses travel through the core by bouncing back and forth on the cladding. As long as the curves in the cable are never too extreme, the light pulses always hit the cladding at an angle, allowing them to be reflected forward through the core. Using cladding on the core allows fiber optic cables to be installed around corners, through walls, and underground.

Digging Deeper

Your Challenge!

Ask an adult to help you explore fiber optics. Make some light-colored gelatin. Once it sets, cut the gelatin into 1-inch (2.5-centimeter) strips. Dim the lights and shine a laser pointer at an angle through a strip of gelatin and see what happens. You might need to adjust the angle of the laser.

Summary

Fiber optics transmit information, such as sound and images, as pulses of light through long strands of glass or plastic. They can send this information around the world in less than one second.

Further Inquiry

Fiber optics transmit pulses of light. The eye transmits wavelengths of light into color. Maybe we should ask:

What are the primary colors?

What Are the Primary Colors?

A primary color is any of a group of colors from which all other colors can be made by mixing. A primary color cannot be produced by mixing two colors together, and the primary colors are combined to produce all the other colors, or hues. Colors can be mixed either by combining colors of light or by combining colored **pigments**.

The primary colors of light are red, blue, and green. They can be added together to produce every color. Look closely at a television screen while it is on. There are tiny dots of red, blue, and green light. In various combinations, these colors produce all the colors seen on the screen.

The primary colors of pigments are red, yellow, and blue. These are the colors used to make dyes, inks, and paints. Pigments absorb some colors of light and bounce others back to the eye. Absorbed colors cannot be seen. Only the colors that bounce back are visible.

❮ Mixing pigment and mixing light are very different. Red and green paint, for example, make brown paint, but red and green light make yellow light. Mixing the three primary colors of light results in white light.

⌄ When all colored pigments are mixed together, no color can be seen and a surface appears black.

Digging Deeper

Your Challenge!

Combinations of primary colors create all other colors. Cut a piece of red cellophane, or plastic wrap, large enough to cover the end of a flashlight. Use an elastic band or tape to hold it in place. Do the same with blue and green cellophane using two additional flashlights. Shine any two flashlights at the same spot on a white piece of paper. Record the color that is created. Do this with different combinations of flashlights. Are you surprised at some of the results?

Summary

Primary colors of light are red, blue, and green. Primary colors of pigment are red, yellow, and blue.

Further Inquiry

Some colors are absorbed by objects, and some colors are reflected off of objects. Maybe we should ask:

What gives objects their colors?

What Gives Objects Their Colors?

Every time a person sees a colored object, some of the light is being reflected, while some is absorbed. The color that is reflected to the eye gives the object its color. The rest of the wavelengths are absorbed into the object. When a person sees something that is green, it means that only the green wavelengths of light are reflected back to their eyes.

⌄ Trees in autumn appear different colors because of a chemical change in the trees. This changes what colors of light are reflected and what colors are absorbed by their leaves.

A pigment in plants called **chlorophyll** absorbs red, orange, yellow, blue, violet, and indigo wavelengths from the Sun. The chlorophyll reflects the green color. This is why many plants appear to be green.

⌄ Some tree leaves, including the copper beech, do not turn green. These trees have enough other pigments to mask their chlorophyll.

Digging Deeper

Your Challenge!

Where do leaf colors come from? Research leaf color pigments and identify the three color pigments that give leaves their color. Create a chart that details each one and its role in contributing to leaf color. Hint: If you read this section closely, you can identify one of the pigments to help you get started.

Summary

The color that is reflected to the eye gives the object its color. The rest of the wavelengths of light are absorbed into the object.

Further Inquiry

Objects get their color because light is reflected or absorbed. Light also passes through some objects. Maybe we should ask:

What is refraction?

How Do People See Light?

Light enters the human eye through a clear covering called the **cornea**, which passes light through the lens. The lens focuses the light on the retina, a layer of light-sensitive cells at the back of the eye. The retina changes the light into signals, which travel through the optic nerve to the brain. The brain reads the signals as an image. For people with perfect eyesight, the images are focused directly on the retina.

Most people do not have perfect eyesight. Some see objects close up fairly well, but things farther away look fuzzy and blurry. This is caused by the **focal point** of the light occurring in the eye before it reaches the retina. This condition is called nearsightedness. Other people see distant objects fairly well, but things seen up close are blurry. This kind of vision is called farsightedness. In this case, the image has a focal point beyond the retina.

Eyeglasses and contact lenses are used to correct nearsightedness and farsightedness. They contain lenses that bend the light to focus properly on the retina. Lenses allow people who are nearsighted and farsighted to see as well as people with perfect vision.

When the cornea and the lens refract light, an upside-down image is formed on the retina.

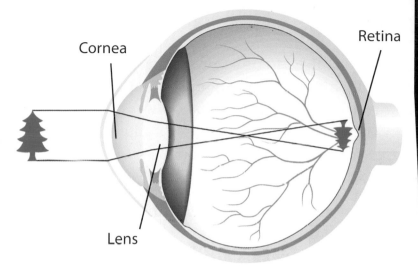

Cornea

Retina

Lens

Most historians believe that the first eyeglasses were produced in Italy around AD 1285. The lenses were shaped like two small magnifying glasses and set into bone, metal, or leather mountings.

Your Challenge!

When light enters the eye, an upside-down image is formed on the retina. Research pinhole cameras, then try to build your own. Using the results of your research, explain why the image appears upside-down, or inverted, inside the pinhole camera.

Summary

Light enters the human eye, is bent by the lens, and then is focused onto the retina. The retina changes the light into signals, which are sent to the brain through the optic nerve and translated into an image.

Further Inquiry

Light waves entering the eye allow people to see. Too much light can damage the eye. Too little light makes it hard to see. Maybe we should ask:

How do eyes adjust to light?

How Do Eyes Adjust to Light?

The human eye is constantly adjusting itself to different levels of light. Usually, the eye adjusts itself without the person even thinking about it. These are involuntary responses by the body. Sometimes, people adjust the amount of light entering the eye using a voluntary response. Squinting, for example, is one way that people use a voluntary response to adjust the amount of light entering the eye.

In order to see things clearly, the amount of light coming from an object must be controlled. In near-darkness, the pupil expands. This allows more light into the eye. In bright sunlight, the pupil contracts, or gets smaller, protecting the eye from being flooded with light. This process takes a moment or two, which is why it takes a while for a person's eyes to adjust to light and dark.

When a person sustains a head injury, the pupils can stop functioning properly. Pupils that are unequal in size are a sign of a brain injury. Another sign is if the pupils are unresponsive to light. When a light is shined directly onto a person's eyeball and the pupils do not change, they may have received a brain injury.

❯ People and objects in dark rooms become easier to see as the eyes adjust to let in more light.

Less Light Is Let In

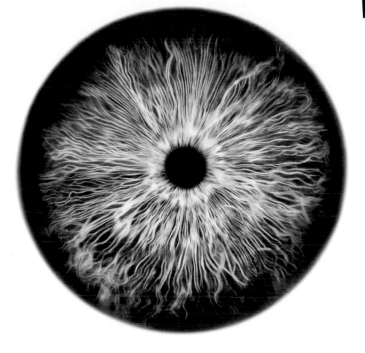

More Light Is Let In

⌃ The iris, or colored part of the eye, controls the size of the pupil.

Your Challenge!

Do the following exercise to observe how the pupil adjusts to different levels of light.

1. Stand in front of a mirror. Observe your pupils.

2. Turn off the lights. Wait 5 minutes.

3. Turn the light back on, and observe your eyes in the mirror.

What happened?

Summary

The eye is constantly adjusting to light levels. The pupil expands to let more light in, and contracts to protect the eye from being flooded by light.

Further Inquiry

Eyes allow us to see objects, but how do they let us see them in color? Maybe we should ask:

How does the eye see color?

How Does the Eye See Color?

Humans use color for many different purposes. How do people tell the difference between all of the different colors in the spectrum? For example, how do people tell the difference between the red signal and the green signal on a traffic light? The retina contains nerve cells called rods and cones. The rods sense brightness and darkness, and allow us to see at night. The cones allow us to see in color. Rods and cones send messages to a type of cell called a ganglion. Ganglion cells then transmit the messages to the brain, where they are turned into images.

There are three types of cones. Red cones are sensitive to red light, green cones are sensitive to green light, and blue cones are sensitive to blue light. Together, these three types of cones allow people to see a large range of different colors.

⌄ Cones in the eye sense colors, such as the colors of beads of glass. The cones send messages through nerves to the brain to see the image.

Some humans are color blind. This means that they cannot perceive as many varieties of color as people with normal vision. Most people who are color blind have trouble distinguishing between reds and greens. About eight percent of males have some form of color blindness. Only 0.5 percent of females are affected by color blindness.

❤ Color blindness is diagnosed using different tests. In one test, a person looks at a set of colored dots and tries to find a pattern, such as a number or letter.

Your Challenge!

Some species of animal have extraordinary eyesight, while other species have very poor eyesight. Create a chart of animals ranking their eyesight and its characteristics. For example, your chart might rank vision from best to worst. Be sure to include humans in your chart as well.

Summary

The eye sees color because of specialized rods and cones that send messages that are transmitted to the brain, where they are turned into images.

Further Inquiry

The brain interprets the messages sent to it by the eyes. Sometimes, the brain can be tricked and gets things wrong. Maybe we should ask:

What are optical illusions?

What Are Optical Illusions?

Seeing does not just involve the eyes. The brain interprets what the eyes see. Sometimes, the brain can be fooled. Optical illusions are pictures that fool the brain. Often the brain is so used to seeing things a certain way that it fills in details that are not really there.

⌄ Optical illusions trick the brain into seeing things which might or might not be real.

The information gathered by the eyes is processed by the brain, and the brain interprets what the eyes see and arrange it into a pattern that makes sense. Optical illusions happen because color, light, and patterns create images that can be deceptive or misleading to the brain. Optical illusions trick the brain into perceiving something differently than it actually is, so what a person sees does not match what is really there.

Digging Deeper

Your Challenge!

Use the internet or other resources to find optical illusions. Develop a procedure to interview several people and test them with the optical illusions you found. Record your results and see if you can identify any patterns.

Summary

Seeing involves more than just light waves and the eye. The brain interprets the messages sent from the eye, and sometimes it can be fooled or misled. This is what occurs during an optical illusion.

Further Inquiry

People use light, the eye, and the brain to see objects. Other devices are used to aid people in seeing objects. Maybe we should ask:

How do lenses help people see?

How Do Lenses Help People See?

People who wear eyeglasses or contact lenses, or anyone who uses a magnifying glass, puts the science of lenses to use. A lens is a curved piece of transparent material used to refract light. Lenses are usually made of glass or plastic, and they have two basic shapes—concave and convex.

A concave lens is thicker around its edges than it is in the middle. These lenses make an object appear smaller and farther away. Concave lenses are sometimes used in cameras. A convex lens is thicker in the middle than at the edges. A convex lens helps to bring an image into focus. It can also be used to make an object appear larger than it actually is. Convex lenses are used in binoculars, cameras, magnifying glasses, microscopes, and telescopes.

❯ Rays of light passing through a concave lens are spread out, or diverged. A concave lens is a diverging lens. Rays of light passing through a convex lens are brought closer together, or converged. A convex lens is a converging lens.

Concave Lens

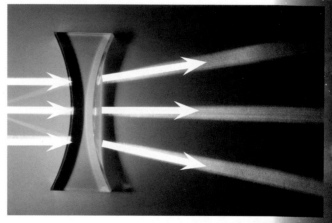

Convex Lens

Many large telescopes, such as the Hubble Space Telescope, use concave mirrors instead of lenses. These powerful telescopes allow scientists to see what happens in deep space.

Digging Deeper

Your Challenge!

Try this experiment to see how lenses bend light. Stretch a piece of plastic wrap on top of a page of newspaper. Place a drop of water on the plastic wrap. Look at the letters through the water droplet. Lift the plastic wrap, and move it closer to and farther from the newspaper. What happens to the size of the letters as you move the plastic wrap?

Summary

Lenses are used to bring light rays closer together or farther apart through refraction. There are two basic types of lenses—convex lenses and concave lenses.

Further Inquiry

Fully understanding light has involved asking many questions and investigating light's properties. Taking all we have learned, maybe we can finally answer:

What is light?

Putting It All Together

Light is a form of energy. The Sun is the main source of light in the solar system. The Sun's light is essential to life on Earth. Light has many properties. It can be reflected, transmitted, absorbed, and refracted. Some light is visible to the human eye. This is the visible light spectrum. Colors in the visible light spectrum include red, orange, yellow, green, blue, indigo, and violet. Other light is invisible to the human eye. Invisible light wavelengths include radio, microwave, infrared, ultraviolet, x-ray, and gamma ray. Together, all the different types of light make up the electromagnetic spectrum. Light is the fastest thing in the universe. The speed of light is about 186,000 miles (299,792 km) per second.

▼ Many people think of light as simply color and brightness, because that is what they see with their eyes every day. Light is really electromagnetic radiation that is both visible and invisible to the human eye.

Where People Fit In

Since ancient times, people have been curious about light: how it acts, its effects, and its many uses. People use light and its energy every day. New ways to use light in technology, in the home, at work, in medicine, and as an alternative energy resource are discovered and developed all the time. Human beings are realizing, now more than ever before, how important it is to understand the relationship between light and the planet Earth that is home to so many different species and organisms.

The process of scientific inquiry allows us to study and understand light and its properties. This, in turn, helps us understand how light affects our lives, our planet, and our understanding of the universe. The more we learn about light, the more questions and answers we discover.

Astronomer

Astronomers spend their time looking at the skies. They study galaxies, the Moon, planets, stars, and the Sun to learn more about the universe. Astronomers work in many different places. They can plan space flights or study information gathered by satellites, telescopes, and observatories. Many people and organizations, such as weather forecasters, NASA, museums, planetariums, and universities, rely on astronomers for information. Becoming an astronomer takes hard work. Most astronomers have a doctoral degree in astronomy. This can take as long as eight years to achieve.

Optometrist

Optometrists, or eye doctors, help people with eye problems. They perform tests on a patient's eyes to find out what prescription they need in order to see better. Optometrists can test for illnesses in the eyes that may cause blindness or other vision problems. When the patient's prescription is determined, the optometrist can then help the person pick out a correct pair of glasses or contact lenses. To be an optometrist, a person must study for many years. Most optometrists begin with a four-year bachelor of science degree from a university. Once this is completed, they must then take a four-year training program at a school of optometry.

Young Scientists at Work

Test Your Knowledge

Test your knowledge of light with these questions and activities. You can probably answer the questions using only this book, your own experiences, and your common sense.

Fact

The length of an object's shadow depends on the location of the light source in relation to the object.

Test

Place an object, such as a glass of milk, on a table. Turn a flashlight on, and move it to different positions in front of the glass of milk while observing the length of the shadow behind the glass of milk.

Predict

Where is the flashlight when you make the following shadows?

   a. the longest

   b. the shortest

   c. the widest

   d. the narrowest

Answers: a. when the light is held low, close to the table b. when the light is held over the top of the glass c. when the light is held very close to the glass d. when the light is held far away from the glass.

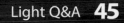

Take a Light Quiz

What are the two types of cells, found in the retina, that see color?

What are the two basic shapes of lenses? What effect does each type of lens have?

Name two important discoveries made by Albert Einstein.

What are the three reactions light can have when it hits an object?

What is the name of the pigment that gives leaves their green color?

Key Words

alternative energy: energy sources that are not based on burning fossil fuels

atoms: the smallest components of an element

chlorophyll: a chemical needed for photosynthesis in plants

composition: what something is made of

cornea: the clear outer covering of the eyeball

electromagnetic energy: energy in the form of electrical or magnetic waves that travel at the speed of light

electromagnetic spectrum: the different wavelengths of light energy, including visible light

focal point: the spot where light rays meet after they are bent by a lens

lenses: clear objects that bend and focus light

magnetic fields: the space around a magnet where the magnet is able to attract metals

particles: very small bits of matter, such as atoms

photons: particles of light

photosynthesis: the process plants use to make their own food from carbon dioxide, water, and sunlight

pigments: a substance that gives an object its color by absorbing and reflecting different types of light

renewable energy: energy that comes from sources that will never run out, such as sunlight or wind

vacuum: a space with no matter in it, not even air

wavelength: the distance between the top of one wave and the top of the wave behind it

Index

Log on to www.av2books.com

AV² by Weigl brings you media enhanced books that support active learning. Go to www.av2books.com, and enter the special code found on page 2 of this book. You will gain access to enriched and enhanced content that supplements and complements this book. Content includes video, audio, weblinks, quizzes, a slide show, and activities.

AV² Online Navigation

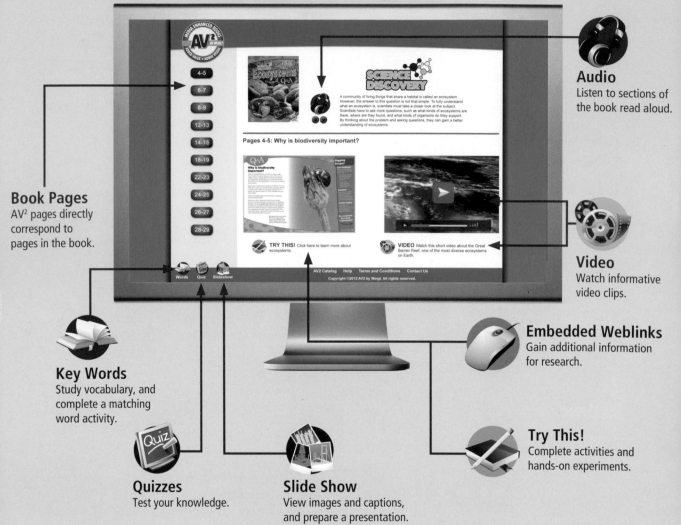

Audio
Listen to sections of the book read aloud.

Book Pages
AV² pages directly correspond to pages in the book.

Video
Watch informative video clips.

Embedded Weblinks
Gain additional information for research.

Key Words
Study vocabulary, and complete a matching word activity.

Try This!
Complete activities and hands-on experiments.

Quizzes
Test your knowledge.

Slide Show
View images and captions, and prepare a presentation.

AV² was built to bridge the gap between print and digital. We encourage you to tell us what you like and what you want to see in the future.

Sign up to be an AV² Ambassador at www.av2books.com/ambassador.

Due to the dynamic nature of the Internet, some of the URLs and activities provided as part of AV² by Weigl may have changed or ceased to exist. AV² by Weigl accepts no responsibility for any such changes. All media enhanced books are regularly monitored to update addresses and sites in a timely manner. Contact AV² by Weigl at 1-866-649-3445 or av2books@weigl.com with any questions, comments, or feedback.